Amelio Marta

By Louisa Tere

AMELIO MARTA

Written by Louisa Tere

©2025, Louisa Tere. All Rights Reserved.

No part of this publication may be reproduced, stored in a retrieval system, or transmitted in any form or by any means: electronic, mechanical, photocopying, recording, scanning or otherwise, without prior written permission from the author.

Library of Congress Control No.: 2025906080

Paperback ISBN: 979-8-9892784-2-8

Illustrations were created with Chatgpt.com.

Give a Salute! provides publishing services according to the specifications of the author. The author approves and retains all responsibilities and rights to the content of this book.

ACKNOWLEDGMENTS

Special recognition to the following educators, mentors, and valued family and friends who continue to implement their vision for a safer and brighter tomorrow as a legacy for our children, with the hope that each voice will be heard.

In alphabetical order:

Christy Bonnani, Paula Cogut, Despina Costa, Cynthia Dafnis, Cheree DiBiccari, Marie Fillippo, Judy Griffin, Maria Katechis, Presbytera Maria Koulianos, Smytha Kumar, Francesca Littleton, Lisa Malakoff, Phyllis Marcus, Wendy Morin, Lynn Nazzaro, Tammy Orrico, Angela Orrico, Achieng Owako, Tatiana Pietris, Anne Prokop, Deb Ripperger, Dr. Lisa Rizopoulos, Liz Ronda, Joyce Scott, Pam Smith, Lauren Stafford, Maria Teleiopoulou, Angie Thrapsimis, Peggy Tsiavos, Allison Valentino, and the countless others who have assisted me on this journey.

A special thank you and appreciation to my exceptional publisher and cherished friend, Catherine Waldron, whose dedication, innovative hands-on assistance, encouragement, and tireless support were invaluable and instrumental in helping me bring Amelio Marta to fruition. I am truly grateful for this collaborative and impactful experience in the hope of making a positive difference in a child's life.

    I would be remiss if I did not acknowledge Melissa Mullahey, Jacob Cascioli, Lauren Stafford, and Mauricio Espinoza for their insight and initial input during this process. With appreciation, thank you for believing in this endeavor.

"In the depths of vulnerability, we can choose to overcome and triumph."   - Louisa Tere

MESSAGE FROM AUTHOR

Amelio Marta has been much anticipated, from conception to, at long last, final rendition. The characters, Amelio and Marta, have astoundingly come to life from heart to storybook portrayal. Their authenticity of interpersonal dynamics and real-time concerns are addressed with self-reflection, honesty, and genuineness.

Amelio Marta brings awareness, insight, and recognition to the emotional complexity of bullying. Let it be clear; **bullying is never okay!** My hope is that this book brings comfort, hope, and insight to hurting hearts and encourages courage in spirit to overcome any mistreatment that may come one's way.

With heartfelt blessings, encouragement, and positiveness, I am sincerely sending life-affirming good wishes.

Warm Regards,

Louisa Tere

DEDICATION

Amelio Marta is dedicated to my son Yianni and to every student and child that has been an integral part of my journey as an educator and counselor. It is also dedicated to everyone who can make a positive difference in who they are and who they aspire to be.

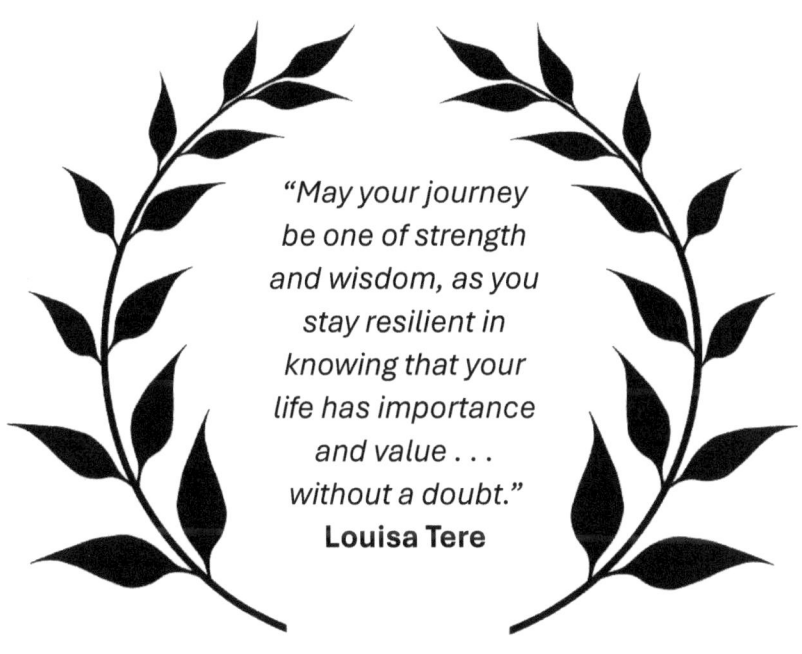

"May your journey be one of strength and wisdom, as you stay resilient in knowing that your life has importance and value . . . without a doubt."
Louisa Tere

PREFACE

It is on us to be the significant difference makers. We are encouraged to always demonstrate positivity, safety, accountability, and appropriate self-control. We are to model an integrity-based mindset of respectfulness, kindness, and overall fairness.

What we say and how we say it matters. Let our voices be strong for those who aren't. Let our actions reinforce that there is no justifiable excuse for bullying or tolerance of mistreatment in any way.

Let us agree that **BULLYING IS NEVER OKAY!**

A new school; a new district.

Dear Diary,

Moving here hasn't been easy, but it's been necessary because of my dad's employment. I hope that his recent promotion will enable him to spend more time with us and will help make this new place feel more like home.

Genuine friends have been hard to come by in the past. I've had to prove myself more times than I'd like to remember. The loneliness and hurt of bad behavior and cruel words from some kids in my previous school have made me realize that I have to be emotionally strong to overcome these circumstances.

There is hope that it will be different in this new school. It's a fresh start, and I'm looking forward to making new friends.

I will not give in to the darkness of lost hope and despair and will do my best to overcome any difficulties that come my way. I will move forward with confidence and anticipation, believing that this year will bring a more positive experience.

AMELIO

Being the new kid once again will be interesting. I'm hoping this time will be better. Maybe it'll be easier to fit in. Maybe the kids will not be so standoffish and will include me and try to get to know me. I hope they will give me a chance. I will be an outsider, for sure, but will do my best to come into this with a positive attitude. Maybe, just maybe, I'll be lucky enough to make at least one really good friend.

    Okay, it's time for me to do this, so here I go. It's the first day in my really big new school. My mom and dad say it will be a great start to my new adventure. I sure hope they're right!

I am Amelio and am ready for this new adventure's positive outcome!

Dear Diary,

Being the new girl at my past school had its difficulties and challenges. It's been hard for our family to move so often. However, I am thankful that my parents and sister continue to always be there for me. Their guidance and love have given me the ability to choose wisely and live with the knowing that I do have worth and purpose.

With each move I've managed to try to make the best of things. However, I still wonder why some friends have truly not turned out to be true friends at all. I'm not sure who to trust and call a friend anymore. It gets so sad and lonely to realize that the actions and words of others can be mean and hurtful.

I have mixed emotions in facing this upcoming unknown. Maybe this time will be different. I hope that my new school will be a fresh start with wonderful and caring relationships. I want to enjoy what the new school year can bring.

MARTA

Today is the first day of school and, once more, I'll be the new girl in class. I'm hoping this time will be different, and that I'll find the right group of friends. Maybe, and I'm hoping, I will make at least one true friend.

Mom and my older sister gave me a helpful pep talk earlier, but I guess I can't hide my nervousness behind a smile. I admit I have mixed emotions and butterflies thinking about all this. I know I can make the best of it; I'm really needing and hoping for an incredible school year.

I am so wanting to finally feel like I belong, so I will get past my nervousness and believe the best is yet to be.

I am Marta, capable and ready to be the best version of me!

Same anxiety;
same fear.
I will try to
adapt.

Hidden insecurity
follows me.
I will do my best.

Internal Battle

Random Behavior

Sense of Failure

Abandoned

Fragile

Unworthiness

Misunderstood

Alone & Defeated

It's not easy . . .
I've been here for a
week now, and I've
tried to fit in.
Once again,
I don't.

It's so
discouraging.
I want to
belong.

BULLIED

So-called friends spit out venom,
cowardly mocking behind social media.

Nocturnal taunting; printed ridicule.

My thoughts are guarded. I try to be invisible.
Why is it so hard to belong?

My words are few. I wish I could disappear.
Why is fitting in so difficult?

I have tried to blend in as if I actually belong, but I know I truly don't. Why am I being bullied? I say very little or nothing at all. I don't make eye contact with those that taunt me. I mask my awkwardness and feelings of aloneness by keeping to myself. I'm rarely ever included in social functions. Why can't they accept me for who I am?

I am not anonymous. I have feelings; I matter. Others look past me as if I don't exist. Their exclusion of me is heartbreaking. Their thoughtlessness and hurtful remarks make me feel inadequate. I do not understand why they treat me so badly. Don't they realize how damaging their words and actions are? Do they even care?

The unkind conduct of others will not
be a roadblock to our success.

There are choices before us.
An unpaved road awaits; it is
meant for each of us to discover.

REALIZATION

I need to be the change.

I must be willing to make the difference.

I do have a lot to offer. I am kind, caring, and have a good sense of humor. I will continue to be strong and not give in to peer pressure or poor decision-making. I will be my very best me and will not give up. I know that I will fit in when I am with the right circle of friends who have the same hopes for a positive outlook and authentic friendship. My life has meaning and importance, and I will no longer blend in where I'm not seen and valued for who I am.

I am Amelio!

For so long, I went through the motions. I stayed in the background and my presence was overlooked for the most part. But no more. I will be seen and heard for who I truly am. I am deserving to be the honest expression of myself—capable, caring, and unique. I will no longer be defined by thoughtless words and insensitive behavior. I will go forth, strong in my decision to overcome social adversity. I am me, and I'll no longer hide.

I am Marta!

I am my
mother's
son—
I am loved.

I am my
father's
daughter—
I am loved.

We will be true to who we are, knowing our lives matter; we deserve to be treated with respect.

We will safeguard our uniqueness.
We have deep-rooted courage.

We will make a difference!
We are the change!

Let's unite in saying **NO** to bullying
and **YES** to acceptance and appreciation
of one another's uniqueness!

REMINDERS

- I can't force a change in others but can strive to be the positive change in my own life.
- I can choose to make a difference with my own words and deeds.
- I will not revel in confrontation or having the last word to prove my sense of worth.

- I will overcome the insecurities of bullying and will let go of the hurt of those who try to diminish me.
- I will reach out for help from a trusted mentor or loved one who facilitates well-being and encourages a healthy, positive, and productive life.
- I will not give up, choosing rather to overcome painful circumstances and stay resilient in my hope.
- I will live a life of triumph and interpersonal healing.

TRUST

T   **Talk**
Talk with authenticity and active listening. Treat the conversation with sincerity, respect, and genuine concern and caring.

R   **Recognize**
Recognize vulnerability and encourage positivity. Offer a proactive resolution. Reach out with your time and availability of resources.

U   **Understand**
Understand feelings and emotions of the situation. Express your understanding with empathy and compassion. Undertake a plan for well-being.

S   **Share**
Share your insight, knowledge, and support in facilitating a safe space for sincere, open, honest, and transparent communication. Share thoughts for a productive solution.

T   **Triumph**
Assist in the triumph of overcoming a sense of defeat and inadequacy. Foster triumphant thoughts for a better and brighter tomorrow.

Family, School, and Society,

We have fallen short in appropriately addressing the fundamental needs of emotional stability and the healthy and positive well-being of our children's safety and mindset. Anxiety, uncertainty, and confusion are not uncommon, along with feelings of loneliness and despair. Mixed emotions of anger and depression can surface, along with thoughts of helplessness and hopelessness. Feeling unseen and lost can escalate to a sense of unworthiness and negativity.

- *Let us remember that our children look to us and to their peers for validation and acceptance.*
- *Let our communication be authentic and not self-serving.*
- *Let our dynamics be that of compassion and genuine caring.*
- *Let us not tolerate mistreatment in any form or ignore the red flags of being bullied and bullying.*
- *Let us be the providers and caretakers that model goodness, goodwill, and confidence in the new day to come.*

NO TO MAYBE

**Bullying is never okay. Bullying is not ever okay.
Being bullied is not okay. Being a bully is not okay.**

No means **NO** to bullying and being bullied.
No means **NO** to accepting this hurtful behavior.
No means **NO** to allowing this aggressive behavior of ill-intent.
No means **NO** to permitting this unacceptable ill-willed behavior.
No means **NO** to tolerating cruelty of words and actions of bullying.
No means **NO** to not recognizing bullying behavior.
No means **NO** to not acknowledging the need for intervention.
No means **NO** to not having available trained staff for counsel and guidance.
No means **NO** to not having literature accessible for insight and bullying awareness.
No means **NO** to not providing positive and healthy resolutions.
Yes means **YES** to encouraging and supporting respectful treatment for everyone.
Yes means **YES** to enforcing rules of safety and well-being.

Let us be sensitive and aware of our role and responsibility in modeling good behavior and fostering the Golden Rule.

REFLECTION

In the process of writing this book on bullying, I have encountered exceptional young individuals who told me of their own painful experiences of having been targets of bullying. They shared how they overcame the barrage of insults, taunts, and social anxiety. Each personal account was one of overcoming the challenges of loneliness, rejection, and feelings of aloneness in having been bullied.

Amelio Marta fosters hope, encouragement, courage, and inner strength. Know that you are not invisible and that you matter as you go forward with confidence that someone cares and understands. Break the silence and seek help and guidance for a positive and healthy resolution on your behalf.

Life is worth living with integrity and respect. Be resilient in your own story of personal success and well-being.

RESOURCES FOR KIDS

DoSomething: Bullying

https://www.dosomething.org/us/causes/bullying

Kids Against Bullying

http://www.pacerkidsagainstbullying.org/

Teens Against Bullying

http://www.pacerteensagainstbullying.org/

Facts for Kids about Bullying

https://www.stopbullying.gov/kids/facts

Bullying: Kid's Hotline

https://kidshelpline.com.au/teens/issues/bullying

Kids Health: Dealing with Bullies

https://kidshealth.org/en/kids/bullies.html

RESOURCES FOR PARENTS

Facts about Bullying
https://www.stopbullying.gov/resources/factshttps://www.stopbullying.gov/resources/what-you-can-do

Research on Bullying/Bullies
https://tarrant.tx.networkofcare.org/kids/library/article.aspx?id=871

Bullying Resource Center
https://www.aacap.org/AACAP/Families_and_Youth/Resource_Centers/Bullying_Resource_Center/Home.aspx

What Parents Can Do
https://www.greatschools.org/gk/articles/what-parents-can-do-about-childhood-bullying/

Cyberbullying Research Center
https://cyberbullying.org/

Stop Bullying Now!
http://www.stopbullyingnow.com/

ABOUT THE AUTHOR

Louisa Tere received her MS degree in Education and Counseling, further completing a post-graduate program in Family Therapy from Long Island University. She worked in an urban multi-cultural school as an educator and a counselor for over 20 years. Her counseling experience also includes working in a residential school facility for "at risk" children, now referred to as "at promise" youth. Her love and dedication for her students and their well-being was rewarding and reciprocated in turn.

Having been an ongoing voice for those whose voices have not been acknowledged, Louisa continues to advocate for those whose voices go unheard.

"All lives have promise, worth, and value. There is no place for bullying. Bullying is definitely not okay…ever!"

www.ingramcontent.com/pod-product-compliance
Lightning Source LLC
Chambersburg PA
CBHW052034030426
42337CB00027B/5006